SHOULD WE LEAVE OUR CHURCHES?

SHOULD WE LEAVE OUR CHURCHES?

A BIBLICAL RESPONSE TO
HAROLD CAMPING

**J. LIGON DUNCAN AND
MARK R. TALBOT**

PUBLISHING
P.O. BOX 817 • PHILLIPSBURG • NEW JERSEY 08865-0817

CONTENTS

INTRODUCTION

In early 2002, religious news services began to report some strange claims by Harold Camping, the co-founder and president of the Family Radio Network. Among others, Christianity Today and World magazines alerted their readers to the fact that Mr. Camping had begun announcing "the end of the church age" both in writing and on his Open Forum program on Family Radio. Meanwhile, impeccable evangelical ministries that broadcast their own programs on Family Radio were finding the content edited without authorization and with all references to the church deleted.

This is not the first time that Camping has landed himself in controversy. In 1992, he published a book arguing that 1994 would be the end of the world and mark the coming of Christ.[1] It wasn't. Not only was Camping shown to be utterly confused in his eschatological exegetical method, but he is also the only self-described amillennialist to so publicly hazard an opinion about the precise timing of Christ's return.

So here we are, ten years later, and Camping has produced another prophetic novelty. What is he saying now? In short, on his weekday evening radio talk show Open Forum and at the Family Radio website, Camping claims that God is no longer blessing and using local churches. In fact, the church age has ended. The institutional church is now under God's curse because of its apostasy. It should disband and its clerical ministries cease. By implication, the sacraments should no longer be administered.[2] True Christians should no longer submit to the authority of any local church body; indeed, obedience to God now requires them to remove themselves from their local churches. God has taken the task of evangelization away from the church and given it to organizations "like Family Radio." (When Camping says this, he fails to mention any ministries other than Family Radio.)

Although (as we shall see) Camping attempts to establish the truth of these claims from Scripture, he comes to this view partly from his analysis of the current church situation:

Certainly, something strange is happening. On the one hand, we see churches everywhere becoming more and more apostate. Yet on the other hand, we see a ministry like Family Radio becoming more and more useful to the Lord in sending the true Gospel into the world.

Virtually every one of us, as we look at the church we attend, and as we look at the other churches in our day, deplore what we are seeing. The worship service has become increasingly a time of entertainment. The preaching seldom, if ever, warns of the imminence of judgment day. Church after church features signs and wonders. Little or no money is available for mission work because of increasing obligations to pay for newer and finer buildings and greater and greater pastors' salaries.

Perhaps one of the most shocking experiences of the true believer within these churches is the rejection he will experience if he contends too strongly for greater purity in doctrine. Indeed, any spiritually minded believer must admit something drastic has happened and is happening in even the most conservative of the churches.

How can it be then that a ministry like Family Radio appears to be increasingly blessed as it is able to share the true Gospel with an increasingly large percentage of the world's population? We do know that there are many prophecies in the Bible that indicate that as the history of the world draws to a close, the congregations and denominations will be increasingly apostate. For example, we have learned in this study that Revelation 13 speaks of a time when Satan, called the beast that comes out of the sea, will rule in the churches through false gospels. In this chapter these churches are called a false prophet that comes out of the earth. These churches have become altogether apostate.[3]

Our purpose in writing is to refute claims and counsel like this. In fact, some months ago, the Alliance of Confessing Evangelicals felt strongly enough to issue this statement:

> The Alliance of Confessing Evangelicals has been gravely concerned about Mr. Camping's claims from their first airing. We, with Christians everywhere, affirm that the church is Christ's bride, which he has promised to cherish and preserve until he comes again. We find Mr. Camping's claims regarding the end of the church age to twist the Scriptures in a way similar to that against which the apostle Peter warns at the end

of his second letter; and so we admonish our fellow Christians, in Peter's words, to take care not to be carried away by these errors and thus lose their own stability. (see 2 Peter 3:16–17)[4]

Indeed, the Alliance has attempted to reason charitably with Camping about this. In April of 2002, the Alliance's Council appointed several representatives to meet with Camping and urge him to acknowledge his errors and turn back from his unbiblical course. This meeting took place in June of 2002, but unfortunately to no avail.

1

OVERVIEW OF CAMPING'S CLAIMS

No matter whether or how far each of us agrees with Camping's assessment of the current scene, his argument is clear:

1. He believes that today's institutional church is completely apostate.
2. He believes that Family Radio is still a beacon of truth.
3. He believes that this situation is predicted and described in Scripture.
4. He believes that the only proper response to this situation is for Christians to leave their churches, huddle together on Sunday in informal groups, and listen to Family Radio.

The specifics of Camping's position continue to evolve, but many of them are found in his online book, The End of the Church Age . . . and After.[1] In outline form, they come to this:

1. Camping sees empirical evidence of the institutional church's apostasy and of God's blessing on Family Radio.

2. He appeals to apocalyptic literature in both the Old and the New Testaments—Revelation 13; 2 Thessalonians 2:1–10; Daniel 8:10–14; Matthew 24:24—to explain the institutional church's apostasy. He claims that the Bible prophesies that the church will become apostate and that these prophecies have come true in our time. Satan is now ruling in the church, and false prophets and false christs are afoot.

3. Yet it is necessary that the gospel go out to all people before Christ can return (see Matt. 24:14). The institutional church was God's delivery system for the gospel for 1,950 years. So how can the gospel go out to all people if the era of the institutional church is now at an end? Why, by means of Family Radio. Family Radio is obviously healthy and blessed. So while the institutional church delivered the gospel for 1,950 years, now technology is going to replace it.

4. But what about the Bible's statements about the church's invincibility and permanency—statements such as Christ's promise in Matthew 16:18 that "I will build my church, and the gates of hell shall not prevail against it"? Camping attempts to undercut these promises by distinguishing between what he calls the "corporate external church" and "all those individuals who personally have become saved."[2] God's curse is on the former. The latter are still "safe and secure."[3]

12

5. In his sixth chapter, Camping attempts to prove that God has rejected the corporate external church. The main feature of his suspect exegesis is what Camping identifies as "the problem of high places." These high places were "places outside of Jerusalem" in Old Testament times "where false God's [sic] were worshipped."[4] With appeal to passages like Leviticus 26:27–34, Camping argues that Old Testament Israel was rejected, destroyed, and exiled because of these high places. This came to pass when first the northern kingdom and then the southern kingdom fell.

6. Israel's fall, Camping claims, foreshadowed God's present judgment on the "corporate external church," which is the "New Testament Israel." In his sixth chapter, Camping identifies some of the corporate external church's current "high places." What are these high places? Camping observes that in "Old Testament days it took serious thought as to how to properly design and build a high place in order to make the overall worship scene more complete."[5] In the New Testament era, it is the same:

> Serious men have carefully thought about teachings they felt were pleasing to God. They reasoned together in solemn meetings such as church councils, consistories and synods. After prayerful consideration, they adopted doctrines which were not always true to the Bible. Some of the erroneous conclusions were even written into and became a part of very prestigious confessions. This was so even though they had arrived at conclusions that were not taught in the Bible. Such conclusions that there can be divorce for fornication, baptismal regeneration, our faith is an instrument that God uses to bring us to salvation, a future millennium, women can pastor a church, universal atonement, our

13

acceptance of Christ as a requirement for salvation, are typical of many doctrines solemnly adopted by churches. But these are high places in that they have come from the exalted minds of men instead of from God.[6]

Camping then declares that God has overlooked these spiritual high places in the church for over 1,950 years, just as he overlooked Israel's high places for "many hundreds of years." But now God's patience has run out, and so his judgment has fallen on the corporate external church.

7. Finally, in his seventh chapter, Camping scours Matthew 24, Mark 13, Revelation 11 and 13, Daniel 7 and 8, 2 Thessalonians 2, and more to prove that we are now in the Great Tribulation and that a central part of that tribulation involves the institutional church's apostasy and the obligation of true believers to flee from it. His instructions are explicit here:

> Now the big question. What are we to do now that we have this information concerning the church?
>
> If the church age has come to an end, what are the believers to do who are members of churches?
>
> Obedience to the command of Luke 21:20–24 can be accomplished in various ways. If a person or family is a member of a church, they can withdraw their membership and fellowship on Sundays with whomever there may be who are of like mind. Such withdrawal may initiate a move by the church to excommunicate. For that individual, this is not a trauma because he has become convinced that the church era has come to an end and the church no longer has any divine authority.

If the individual or family are simply attending a church and are not members, they can stop attending that church but continue to fellowship outside of the church with individuals of like mind.

If a congregation decides to be obedient to this command, they can reorganize their congregation from a church congregation to become a fellowship of believers. The elders will no longer be elders. The deacons will no longer be deacons. The pastor will no longer be pastor. In other words no individuals will have spiritual rule over the congregation.[7]

2

ERRORS AND ISSUES

Camping's errors are too numerous and too serious to be fully answered in a short response.[1] So we shall only address some of the more significant issues.

First and foremost is the unmistakable deficiency in his doctrine of the church. Ecclesiology—or the study of what the Bible teaches about the church—has not been evangelicalism's strong point over the last hundred years. Camping shares this weakness; for him, the visible church, as the institutional form of the kingdom of God, is incidental to God's grand redemptive plan. It is a mere phase, a dispensable mode of operation, and a temporary instrument. This is a far cry from the Bible's true view, as we shall see later.

With that said, some specific features in Camping's presentation of his own view ought to be noted. Some of these features involve theological error. Others involve errors of analysis. And some are peculiar aspects of his approach that may attract those who are inclined to value his opinion for various reasons.

1. A false analysis of the contemporary church situation. Is Camping's description of the contemporary scene correct? To call inaccurate his assertion that "we see churches everywhere becoming more and more apostate" is an understatement. However critical we may be about the church—and the Alliance has been very critical of the churches and denominations of evangelical Protestantism, lovingly so, we hope, but critical nonetheless—Camping's assessment of the current situation is still exaggerated as well as myopic. Both in our country and throughout the southern hemisphere, we find many of God's people in God's churches being encouraged and exhibiting faithfulness to the biblical gospel while confronting great challenges. Camping's claim that present apostasy (to whatever degree it actually exists) warrants concluding that God is finished with the institutional church is wrong in principle. Granted, there are disturbing signs of infidelity in the church, but no amount of such empirical evidence can outweigh God's promises to preserve his Son's bride and perfect her for his coming.

2. A dubious appeal to the apocalyptic. For a long time Christians have been making big mistakes when they place themselves and their times in the final stages of biblical prophecy fulfillment. (Incidentally, this is a key component of almost every cult—seeing itself as playing a major role in the end-time scenario.) Camping, fresh from the public embarrassment of wrongly predicting what the Son of God himself explicitly said could not be predicted—namely, the timing of his second coming—is now back to help us understand biblical teaching about the church in the end times. Having missed

18

what the Bible says about the Son, he is now going to teach us what it says about the Son's bride—the church. Humility alone should dictate that he keep silent about such things, after bringing such confusion to believers.

3. Allure for the disaffected. Camping's views are likely to appeal to many who are deeply disappointed with the organized church. Much of what he cites as evil is indeed so: entertainment substituted for worship, unfaithful preaching, worldly expenditures of church resources, and bad theology. Of course, his assessment of what is bad theology often reveals his own bad theology. But his argument is likely to draw the interest of those who have been alienated from the church. His views may be adopted by some as a way of justifying their own contempt for this or that local church and as a "biblical" excuse to disengage from all their church obligations. To these, we would simply say, with Albert Mohler, "You have to love the church, before you can reform the church." God has not called us to love perfected saints in perfect communions in this fallen world. He calls us to love sinful saints in congregations that often fall far short of God's standards for his redeemed people. In John 13, Jesus himself explicitly calls us to this task. Professing believers ignore his call at their own peril.

4. A deficient view of the church. Camping possesses a very inadequate view of the church's purpose. He sees it basically as a delivery system that exists primarily or only to evangelize. Since we can now evangelize through technologies like radio and the Internet, there is consequently no longer a need for the church, he says. Such a stunted view of the church is, frankly, staggering. It ignores the church's first and foremost mission: to bring glory to God. Whatever

the church does in missions and evangelism is secondary to that. As John Piper says:

> Missions is not the church's ultimate goal. Worship is. Missions exist because worship doesn't. Worship is ultimate—not missions—because God is ultimate, not man. When this age is over and the redeemed fall on their faces before the throne of God, missions will be no more. It is a temporary necessity, but worship abides forever.[2]

Camping's view of the church also confuses what the church is with what it does. Indeed, he reduces what the Bible says the church does to just one thing—evangelism. Astute readers, not to mention good historians, will not miss this clear hallmark of old-line fundamentalism in Camping's teaching.

5. Technophilia. Camping appears to be anti-modern with his contempt for culturally driven teachings and influences on the organized church. But when it comes to technology, he is quintessentially modern. He assumes that technology can replace missionaries and churches in disciple-making and that a Bible study with superficial fellowship around a Bose Wave Radio can replace mutual accountability and submission to spiritual authority in Christian sanctification. The organizational church's demise does not daunt him— we've got radio, he says. This is a uniquely modern view of things. One of the distinctive myths of modernity, many sociologists have observed, is what has been called "rationalization" (rationalization is the intellectual/worldview consequence of technophilia, that is, love of and confidence in technology). This hopelessly optimistic view that technology can solve all human problems is typical of moderns. In

the modernistic worldview, God and nature have now been replaced by technology and technique. What is real and valuable can be classified, calculated, controlled, predicted, quantified, and produced. There is a "how to" for everything meaningful—and technology has replaced the human and divine. Camping falls right in line with this myth when he assumes that technology can replace the local church in the life of believers.

6. A nonincarnational view of gospel ministry. This leaves us with a nonincarnational view of the gospel ministry of reconciliation.[3] Camping's view of the church's dispensability implies that people need little more than information to attain life and salvation. So let's broadcast the truth—as he sees it—worldwide and that will do just fine. No missionaries, no public professions, no submission to the body, no community, no pastors, no ordinances, and no obligations. Just me, Jesus, my Bible, and Family Radio. This is individualism, pietism, and separatism with a vengeance. Jesus saw it very differently. His disciples were to go into all the world to make disciples, baptizing them—which identified them as part of the visible church—and teaching them—which made the visible church, and especially its local expression, the locus of discipleship (see Matt. 28:19–20 and Acts 2:41–42). He, through his Spirit, appointed elders to shepherd his people (see Acts 20:28) and deacons to serve as mercy ministers (see Acts 6:1–6). The church would thus literally "enflesh" his love command (see John 13:34). And, accordingly, Jesus said that humanity's observation of our own mutual accountability and love in the context of the church community would be essential to our witness to the world. "By this all men will know that you are My disciples, if you have love for one another" (John 13:35 NASB).

21

All of this is lost in the blast of Camping's "Great Tribulation" with its requirement that believers now flee from their churches. Jesus' commission to his disciples in Matthew 28 requires that word and deed, faith and love, heart and community be displayed in a context of mutual accountability in a local church body that reflects the divine marks of the church. This is how God's designs in evangelism may be fulfilled. To be sure, faith comes by hearing (see Rom. 10:17), but the context of such hearing is a community of disciples who have embraced God's incarnational vision for the life of the body of Christ.

7. An improper movement from experience to Scripture. Another weakness of Camping's view is the bizarre way in which he attempts to justify his own peculiar diagnosis and interpretation of the state of the contemporary church and of the role of Family Radio in God's eternal plan by assigning that diagnosis and interpretation to a prophetic source. Looking around, he sees declension, unfaithfulness, and apostasy in the churches. He also avers that Family Radio is doing well. Now, there is nothing subtle or seriously reflective about that kind of judgment concerning the current situation. Nevertheless, with it firmly in mind Camping goes to Scripture to validate and explain it. He wants to find his assessment of the current situation in the Bible—and, not surprisingly, he does! This is an inappropriate way to relate experience and Scripture. Of course, there are proper ways to move from experience to Scripture. For example, we may wonder about God's providence in our lives. So we turn to Scripture to see both what it teaches outright about that topic as well as what it implies about it in passages on how God dealt with his people in the past (see Rom. 15:4; 1 Cor. 10:6, 11). But when we do this, our desire is not—like Camp-

ing's—to find our own unique circumstance prophetically encoded in sacred writ. That is the stuff of narcissism. Rather, we go to Scripture to understand the general principles about providence that God's Word reveals so that we may know how, in general, we ought to respond to his providential workings now. This is different from what Camping has done in several ways: (1) it seeks to understand God's revealed will and does not attempt to force a pre-interpretation of his secret will onto Scripture;[4] (2) it is humble and does not seek to plop ourselves into the middle of the latest plotline from Left Behind; and (3) it is just as interested in the didactic sections of Scripture as it is in its prophetic ones (while Camping's sole focus is on predictive prophecy).

8. A false dichotomy between the "corporate external church" and unchurched "true" believers. As we have already noted, Camping has come up with a new distinction in his doctrine of the church. He speaks of the corporate external church that has now come to an end and of true believers, all of whom should now leave the corporate external church. Consequently, to quote to him passages about the New Testament church makes absolutely no dent in his argument because he applies all of those passages only to individual true believers and not to the local or visible church. He claims that the corporate external church with its orders and ordinances (ministers, elders, deacons, sacraments, the great commission, government, discipline, and more) has ended. It doesn't exist anymore—its era is over. Now Jesus' promises to the church and the instructions in the book of Hebrews concerning Christians assembling together are intended for individual believers meeting in fellowship groups with no preachers, no officers, no sacraments, and the like. Yet there is not even one shred of direct

evidence for this bifurcation in the New Testament. And Camping gives us none. He just asserts it on the basis of his very odd allegorical interpretation of the Scriptures (see point 11, below).

9. Individualism. There is also a marked individualism in Camping's theology. Individualism, whether it is embraced deliberatively or unreflectively, privileges the individual over society. Society is no more than a voluntary bond between individuals—the very sort of bond that Camping encourages in his fellowship groups. All of this is characteristic of the worst of evangelicalism. For Camping, the loss of the church is sad but unimportant. Christians can get along just fine without it. This is a modern myth that plays itself out in the all-too-common view that the communion of the saints and the local church are optional and incidental to Christian experience. This is alien both to Scripture (see Rom. 12:4–5; 1 Cor. 12:12–28; Eph. 4:1–16; Col. 3:15–16; Heb. 10:24–25) and to historic Christian thought, whether it is expressed in Augustine's famous dictum on the necessity of the church—"He cannot have God for his Father who refuses to have the church for his mother"—or in the Westminster Confession of Faith's assertion that outside the visible church "there is no ordinary possibility of salvation" (chapter 25, section 2).

10. A misapplication of his "high places" doctrine because of a failure to appreciate Jeremiah 31. Camping's argument for the end of the church age fails to appreciate the discontinuity found in Scripture between the old and the new covenants (see 2 Cor. 3; Heb. 8:6–9:28). He draws a parallel between the destruction of Israel because of her disobedient false worship and the "Great Tribulation" in which,

he claims, God rejects the corporate external church. Yet even if his exposition of God's dealings with Israel under the old covenant is correct, he has failed to take into consideration a promise at the heart of the new covenant prophecies found in Jeremiah, Isaiah, Ezekiel, and the later prophets. This is God's promise concerning the permanency of the new covenant. Jeremiah says:

> Behold, the days are coming, declares the LORD, when I will make a new covenant with the house of Israel and the house of Judah, not like the covenant that I made with their fathers on the day when I took them by the hand to bring them out of the land of Egypt, my covenant that they broke, though I was their husband, declares the LORD. But this is the covenant that I will make with the house of Israel after those days, declares the LORD: I will put my law within them, and I will write it on their hearts. And I will be their God, and they shall be my people. . . . For I will forgive their iniquity, and I will remember their sin no more. (Jer. 31:31–34; cf. Ezek. 36:22–31)

Here God is declaring through Jeremiah that the new covenant, in contrast to the old, will be permanent and unbreakable and will result in the realization of the primordial covenant promise of everlasting fellowship with God (see Ex. 6:2–8; 1 Thess. 4:17; Heb. 10:5–25; Rev. 21:1–7). And even though the New Testament recognizes a two-stage realization of this fulfillment—the "already" of our present full acceptance with God (see Rom. 5:1–2, 10; Eph. 2:11–19) and the "not yet" of our final perfection in Christ (see Rom. 8:18–25; 1 Cor. 13:9–12; 15:50–55; 1 John 2:28–3:3; Rev. 3:5)—it nevertheless clearly indicates that

25

where old covenant Israel fell short, the church will not. Camping, however, is oblivious to this truth.

11. Gnostic tendencies. Camping's allegorical interpretation of the Scriptures approaches the Bible like a mystery novel or a perplexing puzzle.[5] This pattern of sleuth-like hermeneutics, of finding almost undetectable clues in arcane places and then using them as the key to understanding the final unfolding of all things, reveals his Gnostic tendencies.[6] Those with a hankering to know secret things are likely to be attracted to Camping's fantasies.

12. A strange set of church "high places." Camping seems determined to offend as many Christian traditions as possible in his eclectic examples of the church's false teachings and practices—what he calls its "high places." Teachings sometimes held and practices sometimes evident in Baptist, Lutheran, Reformed, Presbyterian, Anglican, Independent, Bible, and Charismatic circles (and more!) are all taken to be definitive evidence of church apostasy, including worship as entertainment, failure to preach the final judgment, signs and wonders, overpaid pastors, too many building programs, fornication as a legitimate ground for divorce, baptismal regeneration, faith as the instrument of justification, premillennialism, women preachers, and universal atonement. Some of these doctrines and practices are perfectly orthodox, while others involve relatively serious deviations from what God has called his church to be. So the very nature of Camping's list calls for a comment: Camping has charted his own unique set of "orthodox" doctrines and practices, which is not unexpected in someone who thinks and argues in a profoundly individualistic, anticreedal, and anticonfessional way. Rather like the Pharisees, he seems to

26

be deciding just what constitutes the weightier matters of the law.

13. Appeals to futurist readings of biblical prophecy. Another curious irony in Camping's thought: while he decries premillennialism as a mark of apostasy, his own spiritualized amillennialism is profoundly futurist in its interpretation of prophecy. Prophetic Scripture passages that most mainstream evangelical exegetes see as already having been fulfilled in our Lord's incarnation or in the destruction of Israel in 70 A.D. or in some other way, Camping cites as being fulfilled now or in the near future. This can make some of his arguments seem more plausible to laypeople who have been influenced by an unsophisticated presentation of dispensationalism in their own church traditions. Even his use of the term "church age"—not a historic usage in Christian theology but familiar to the Scofield tradition—will appeal to them. Yet this actually reveals the profound internal inconsistencies in Camping's eschatological thought.

14. Parallels with other historical separatist movements. Finally, Camping's call to "come out and be separate" will strike many discerning students of Christian history as familiar. At times of great transition, unrest, and spiritual decay in the church's life, calls have always arisen for people to leave it. All the great American cults and sects—Mormonism, the Jehovah's Witnesses, Christian Science, Adventism, the Campbellites, etc.—reflect this tendency. The thinking goes something like this: the church is hopelessly flawed; the creeds are merely man-made traditions; only we are being truly biblical; therefore, we alone have the truth—so we must come out from the historic church and start afresh. The Reformation era saw its own version of this kind of sep-

aratism among some extreme Anabaptists, but this was never the magisterial Reformers' spirit. They loved the church and desired to see it reformed according to Scripture. Indeed, they recognized that the best of the church's history, beliefs, and practices were already thoroughly biblical. So, rather than despising and rejecting the history of the church, they argued that not only Scripture but also early church history was on their side in the debate of what God wanted his church to be.

3

A BIBLICAL REPLY

Harold Camping attempts to establish the truth of his claims about the end of the church age by arguing for them from Scripture. Consequently, no answer to those claims can be complete without rebutting this argument that he supposedly gets from the Scriptures.

Most generally, we note that the very concept of a "church age" owes more to the dispensational tradition of biblical interpretation than to historic Christian theology. The greatest Christian theologians of the ages have never taken Scripture to view the church as a mere passing phase. Rather, from the perspective of the history of redemption as we find it in the Scriptures, the church is the culminating institutional form of the kingdom of God on earth. Camping's argument is so outlandish in substance, coming from someone already discredited as a reliable guide to prophetic interpretation, that it is hard to conceive how it has gained any attention at all—except that Camping has a chain of radio stations on which to propagate it. A cursory study of the

Bible's clear, positive teaching on the church should inoculate anyone to the appeal of Camping's conjectures. A mere rudimentary knowledge of what the Bible actually says about God's people, Christ's body, and his bride is enough to see through Camping's teachings.

"When we take God for our God," Matthew Henry once said, "we take his people for our people." The church, in other words, is a reality that should concern every Christian. Yet in contemporary evangelicalism no doctrine needs more exposition than the doctrine of the church. In the Bible, the church is of first importance; indeed, it is only through participating in it that God's Old Testament people are made perfect (see Heb. 11:39–40). Yet we Westerners often take individuals to be primary. And so, assailed by such individualism, as well as by anti-authoritarianism and subjectivism, we desperately need to recover a biblical and historical appreciation for what it means to be the Lord's corporate people, the body of Christ.

Biblical Truths about the Church

Let us begin our survey of what Scripture says about the church by considering what the apostle Paul writes to the Ephesians:

Therefore remember that at one time you Gentiles in the flesh, called "the uncircumcision" by what is called the circumcision, which is made in the flesh by hands— remember that you were at that time separated from Christ, alienated from the commonwealth of Israel and strangers to the covenants of promise, having no hope and without God in the world. But now in Christ Jesus you who once were far off have been brought near by the blood of Christ. For he himself is our peace, who has made us both one and has broken down in his flesh the dividing wall of hostility by abolishing the law of commandments and ordinances, that he might create in himself one new man in place of the two, so making peace, and might reconcile us both to God in one body through the cross, thereby killing the hostility. And he came and preached peace to you who were far off and peace to those who were near. For through him we both have access in one Spirit to the Father. So then you are no longer strangers and aliens, but you are fellow citizens with the saints and members of the household of God, built on the foundation of the apostles and prophets, Christ Jesus himself being the cornerstone, in whom the whole structure, being joined together, grows into a holy temple in the Lord. In him you also are being built together into a dwelling place for God by the Spirit.

For this reason I, Paul, a prisoner for Christ Jesus on behalf of you Gentiles—assuming that you have heard of the stewardship of God's grace that was given to me for you, how the mystery was made known to me by revelation, as I have written briefly. When you read this, you can perceive my insight into the mystery of Christ, which was not made known to the sons of men in other generations as it has now been revealed to his holy apostles and prophets by the Spirit. This mystery is that the Gentiles are fellow heirs, members of the same body, and partakers of the promise in Christ Jesus through the gospel.

Of this gospel I was made a minister according to the gift of God's grace, which was given me by the working of his power. (Eph. 2:11–3:7)

When we read this passage in context, we find Paul to be making at least six points. First, Gentiles were once excluded from participation in God's family. Second, believing Gentiles (see Eph. 1:13) have now been brought into that family by the blood of Christ.[1] Third, God's eternal purpose (see Eph. 1:3–10) has always been to create one people to be his people. In the Old Testament they were called Israel; in the New Testament they are the church, which is the body of Christ (see Eph. 1:22–23). Fourth, it is God's divine purpose to bring together both Jew and Gentile into this one body— one household (see Eph. 2:19)—and make them one people, his people. Fifth, the divine purpose is accomplished through union with Jesus Christ because when anyone is "in Christ," then he or she is "joined" or "built" together with all who are "in Christ." Sixth, these truths about the church are a mystery in the biblical sense—that is, they are something that was once concealed but is now revealed. So although the church (as we shall see) was prophetically foretold in a shadowy way in the Old Testament, it did not come to light and realization until the New Testament's age of the Spirit.

From these six points, we realize at least three great truths about the church. First, the doctrine of the church is grounded in the doctrine of the believer's union with Christ. Paul makes it magnificently clear that when we are united to Christ, we are then united to the rest of God's people. This passage makes it incontestable that the church, as God's people, is not just an afterthought or an addendum to God's saving purposes; it is central to his glorious and eternal plan.

Second, the doctrine of the church is grounded in the doctrine of the covenant of grace, which Paul refers to in this passage as the "covenants of promise." The body of Christ is the New Testament covenant community—the visible realization of the one people of God. Scripture is clear that the heart of God's gracious promises to Abraham and his spiritual heirs has always consisted in God's not merely saving individuals but also making them into—and cherishing them as—his one covenant people (see Gen. 12:1–2; Ex. 6:2–7; Lev. 26:3–13; 2 Chron. 7:11–18; Isa. 51:1–16; Jer. 11:1–5; 13:11; 30:18–22; Zech. 8:1–8; Matt. 2:6; Rom. 9:22–26; 2 Cor. 6:16).

Third, the doctrine of the church is grounded in what is formally known as the doctrine of the heavenly session of Jesus Christ. This is the doctrine—heralded by our Lord himself (Matt. 26:64), declared to be a fact by the apostle Peter during his sermon at Pentecost (see Acts 2:33–36; cf. 5:31), and explicitly acknowledged by Paul in Ephesians 1:20—of Christ's now being seated at the right hand of God the Father Almighty (see Rev. 3:21).[2] The New Testament announces this as the fulfillment of the Old Testament prophecy: "The LORD said to my LORD: 'Sit at my right hand, until I make your enemies your footstool' " (Ps. 110:1; see not only Acts 2:34–35 but also Mark 16:19 and Heb. 1:3 with Heb. 1:13). But why is this doctrine important? What is the significance of Christ's now being seated at God the Father Almighty's right hand?

It means that—with his incarnation, life, passion, death, resurrection, and ascension now behind him—Jesus has completed his earthly mission of making purification for sins (see Heb. 1:3) and consequently has received what God, through David's words in Psalm 110, had promised to give to him once his earthly work was done. God the Father has now exalted him above all created rule and authority and power and dominion—indeed, "above every name that is named, not only in this age but also in the one to come" (Eph. 1:21; cf. Matt. 28:18; 1 Peter 3:22; Phil. 2:5–11). In seating him at his right hand (see Eph. 1:20), the Father has "put all things under [Christ's] feet" and has given him "as head over all things to the church, which is his body, the fullness of him who fills all in all" (Eph. 1:22–23). As Calvin comments, to say that Christ is seated at the right hand of the Father means that

> Christ was invested with lordship over heaven and earth, and solemnly entered into possession of the government committed to him—and that he not only entered into possession once for all, but continues in it, until he shall come down on Judgment Day.[3]

With Christ's heavenly session, a new era has begun, one in which he—by virtue of his completed earthly work—is already ruling and through which he will surely bring all things to their proper fulfillment and completion. The church on earth is to be the visible manifestation of Christ's heavenly rule (implied in Eph. 1:22–23). In Ephesians 4, Paul says that when Christ ascended into heaven and led captivity captive, he gave gifts to men that manifest and prove that he is reigning at God the Father's right hand. But what gifts did he give? Church officers! Yes, that's right! Divinely called apostles, prophets, evangelists, pastors, and teachers who have been given for the edification of the church (see Eph. 4:11–13; cf. 1 Cor. 12:28; Rom. 12:4–7).[4] Now, this tells us at least two things. First, if Christ has given us church officers such as elders and pastors and teachers, then we must need them.[5] And secondly, godly church officers are evidence and proof that Christ is indeed now head over all things and the king of his people—the new Israel, his church (see Matt. 21:5; Luke 23:2; Acts 17:7).

None of these great truths about the church seem to have occurred to Camping. He treats individual texts about the church in isolation from their contexts and without keeping this larger web of biblical teaching about the church in mind. Yet keeping these great truths about the church in mind is essential to grasping where Camping has erred.

The Meaning of *Church*

Moreover, when we survey the various uses of the biblical words for church in the Old and New Testaments, we find that Camping's crucial distinctions between, for example, the corporate external church and true or spiritually minded believers are illegitimate and unjustified.

Our word church probably comes from the Greek kyriakon (meaning "the Lord's house"), which the post-apostolic authors used to refer to a place of Christian worship. In the New Testament the Greek word is ekklēsia, which is synonymous with the Hebrew qhal in the Old Testament. Both ekklēsia and qhal mean "an assembly."

The word ekklēsia is used in the following senses in the New Testament: for an assembly in the ordinary nontechnical sense of that word (see Acts 19:32, 39, 41); for a group of Christians meeting together as a church in someone's house (see Rom. 16:5; 1 Cor. 16:19; Col. 4:15; Philem. 1:2);[6] for all Christians in a particular city, whether or not they all worship together, such as "the church in Jerusalem" (Acts 8:1; cf. 15:22) or "the church at Antioch" (see Acts 13:1) or "the church of God that is in Corinth" (1 Cor. 1:2) or "the church in Ephesus" (Rev. 2:1); for all professing Christians throughout the world (see 1 Cor. 15:9; Gal. 1:13; Matt. 16:18); and for all the redeemed or for all those whom God the Father has given to Christ the Son—that is, for the invisible "catholic" or universal church of all time (see Eph. 5:23, 25, 27, 29; Heb. 12:23).

These uses suggest that the term church has at least four legitimate uses. First, there is the local church—that is, a local body of believers gathered together as a church (see Matt. 18:20 along with Rom. 16:5 and Col. 4:15) or a localized group of churches, such as "the churches of God in Christ Jesus that are in Judea" (1 Thess. 2:14). Second, there is the organized church—that is, a group of perhaps geographically diverse church congregations that acknowledge some common leadership (see Acts 15). Third, there is the visible church—that is, the whole body of those who profess Christ throughout the world, along with their children (see 1 John 2:19; John 13:10).[7] And fourth, there is the universal or invisible church—that is, the whole body of God's faithful people, whether they are in heaven or on earth (see Eph. 2:21).

Camping creates his own categories for characterizing the church—for instance, Scripture never refers to the corporate external church—and thus evades having to grapple with the New Testament's detailed teaching about it. In particular, he cannot produce from the Bible one verse that actually teaches his view that there will come a time when true or spiritually minded Christians ought to abandon their local churches and form mere fellowships of believers that have no pastors, elders, and teachers, and that exercise no discipline.[8]

Biblical Images of the Church

We have already noted that Camping's view confuses what the church is with what it does. Scripture teaches that the church is the people of God (see 1 Peter 2:9–10), the body of Christ (see 1 Cor. 12:27), Christ's bride (see 2 Cor. 11:2),

God's building (see 1 Cor. 3:9), the earthly outpost of God's kingdom (see Rev. 1:6), God's family,[9] God's flock (see Acts 20:28–29), and so on. It says that the church does at least the following things: it worships (see Acts 13:1–2); it faithfully preaches and teaches God's Word (see Acts 2:42; 1 Cor. 4:17; Col. 1:24–28; 3:16; 1 Tim. 1:3–4; 2 Tim. 2:2; 4:1–2; Titus 2:1; 1 Peter 1:23–25), administers the sacraments,[10] and carries out church discipline (see 1 Cor. 5; 1 Tim. 1:20; 5:20; Rev. 2:20); it shares life (see Acts 2:42; Eph. 5:19–20; 6:21–22; 1 Thess. 5:11, 14; Heb. 10:24–25; 13:1; 1 Peter 4:8–9; 1 John 1:3, 7), serves (see Matt. 20:25–28; Rom. 12:7; Gal. 5:13–14; Heb. 9:14; 1 Peter 4:10–11), and witnesses by means of evangelism (see Eph. 4:11; 2 Tim. 4:5), missions (see Matt. 28:19; Mark 16:15; Luke 24:47–48; Acts 1:8), and acts of mercy (see Luke 6:36; Rom. 12:8; James 2:12–13; 3:17; Jude 1:23). Camping says virtually nothing about what the church is and then reduces what the church does to just one task: evangelism. For him, the church exists as a means to just one end.

To reveal the utter deficiency of Camping's ecclesiology, we now examine a few more biblical teachings concerning the church as God's people and as Christ's body. As we do, the folly involved in Camping's announcement of the end of the church age will be clear.

We will go to those biblical passages where God is openly and obviously talking about his church—rather than to difficult prophetic passages as Camping does, where he finds clues about an alleged end-time plan for the church. In developing his doctrine of the end of the church age, Camping ignores one of the main rules of correct scriptural interpretation: that we should use the clearer passages of Scripture to help us interpret the less clear passages. It only makes sense, if we want to understand God's concept of the church, to start with those places in Scripture where God is telling us, clearly and directly, who she is, what she does, and why she exists.

The Church as God's People

In the Scriptures, the church fulfills God's promises to gather a people to himself. As Bruce Milne says, "God's relationship with his people is the central theme of the Old Testament, expressed in the repeated declaration 'I will be your God, and you will be my people' " (see Ex. 6:7; Lev. 26:12; Jer. 7:23; 11:4; 30:22; Ezek. 36:28).[11] At the Exodus, God declared that if the Israelites would obey his voice and keep his covenant, then they would be his "treasured possession among all peoples" (Ex. 19:5). Yet they disobeyed him and broke his covenant again and again. God then, through his Old Testament prophets, promised to make a new covenant with Israel, a covenant that would not be like the conditional covenant that he had made with their fathers on the day when he "took them by the hand to bring them out of the land of Egypt" (Jer. 31:32), but "an everlasting covenant" (Jer. 32:40; cf. 32:37–41). This new covenant would involve his putting his law within them and writing it upon their hearts so that they—by means of the gift of his Holy Spirit dwelling within them (see Ezek. 36:27; cf. Ps. 51:7–11)—would practice heartfelt obedience (see Jer. 31:31–34; Ezek. 36:22–32; cf. 11:17–20). The New Testament then proclaims that this new covenant has been struck and the promises attached to it have begun to be fulfilled. God, through Christ's finished work of redemption (see Heb. 4:14, 16; 7:11–8:13;[12] 9:11–15, 23–28; 10:5–18), is now in this New Testament era gathering together a "people for his own possession" (Titus 2:14; 1 Peter 2:9; cf. Rev. 21:3). Because he has given them his Spirit (see Acts 2:33; cf. John 16:7), they are even now "zealous for good works" (Titus 2:14; cf. Eph. 2:10).[13] As Paul makes clear, the benefits of Christ's earthly work are available to all who believe, Jew and Gentile alike (Eph. 2:11–3:7). So Paul calls this one new people, gathered from both Jews and Gentiles, "the Israel of God" (Gal. 6:16).

Camping emphasizes, correctly, that the church is the New Testament Israel. But God's covenant with his people in the New Testament era is decisively different from his covenant with the nation of Israel in the Old Testament era. And that difference means that Camping's primary parallel between Old Testament Israel and the New Testament church is illegitimate. Camping's entire argument that God has abandoned the church because of her apostasy turns on the assumption that God's keeping his covenant with his church is conditioned on their continued obedience, just like the conditional covenant he had with Old Testament Israel. But that assumption is false! The old and the new covenants differ at precisely this point: the old covenant was contingent and temporary, the new covenant is "everlasting" (Jer. 32:40), and "permanent" (2 Cor. 3:11). Paul tells us that the covenant that God struck with the nation of Israel at Mount Sinai after the Exodus was a "ministry of death, carved in letters on stone" (2 Cor. 3:7). It has now been "brought to an end" (2 Cor. 3:7). The author of Hebrews tells us that the old covenant's faults were the occasion for the new covenant (see Heb. 8:7), a covenant that is "better" than the old covenant "since it is enacted on better promises" (Heb. 8:6). It is enacted on the promises that God the Father made to God the Son before time began, promises that include giving to the Son his own people (see John 17:2,

6) and giving him all authority in heaven and on earth (see Matt. 28:18), including the authority to pour out the Holy Spirit to save and sanctify those who trust in him (see Acts 2:33 with John 3:5–6 and 2 Thess. 2:13; 1 Peter 1:2).[14] The new covenant, inaugurated with Christ's blood (see Heb. 9:11–28), ushers in a new era, the era of "the ministry of the Spirit" (2 Cor. 3:8) that, unlike the ministry of death inherent in the old covenant, secures an "eternal redemption" (Heb. 9:12) for those who believe.

In the Old Testament era, God's continued blessing upon the nation of Israel was linked to their continued obedience; and so God said to Moses:

> Thus you shall say to the house of Jacob, and tell the people of Israel: You yourselves have seen what I [God] did to the Egyptians, and how I bore you on eagles' wings and brought you to myself. Now therefore, if you will indeed obey my voice and keep my covenant, you shall be my treasured possession among all peoples, . . . and you shall be to me a kingdom of priests and a holy nation. (Ex. 19:3–6)

But in the church era, the conditional element in God's covenant with his people disappears. In spite of what Camping says, the church era will not come to an end because God has promised it won't (see Matt. 16:18). The writer to the Hebrews summarizes the crucial theological point that Camping has missed: Christ "is the mediator of a new covenant, so that those who are called may receive the promised eternal inheritance, since a death" (Heb. 9:15)—Christ's death, the death of the innocent "Lamb who was slain" (Rev. 5:12)—"has occurred that redeems them from the transgressions committed under the first covenant." The phrase "those who are called" in this quotation refers to God's New Testament people, the church. The church receives this promised eternal inheritance and in this way is decisively different from Old Testament Israel. God's dealings with his New Testament people—God's dealings with his church—are thus decisively different from his dealings with the nation of Israel.

The Church as the Body of Christ

The point we have just made should be enough, even standing alone, to show that Camping's doctrine of the end of the church age is unscriptural. It is based on a demonstrably unbiblical—indeed, a profoundly un-Christian[15]— assumption. But there is more. As we delve more deeply into another biblical term for the church, we find that Camping's distinction between the corporate external church and true (or spiritually minded) believers cannot be sustained, nor can his claim that true believers should now leave their churches and form fellowships that have no church officers.

This is the biblical description of the church as "the body of Christ." Paul uses this image to bring into sharp focus the profound interdependence that each individual Christian has on every other Christian (see Rom. 12:4–5; 1 Cor. 12:12–27), as well as what each Christian has in common with all other Christians—namely, the relationship that each of us has as a member of this body to Jesus Christ as the body's "head" (see Eph. 1:22–23; 4:15–16; 5:21–32; Col. 1:18; 2:19).[16]

When Camping distinguishes between the corporate external church and true believers, he is in effect making a kind of visible/invisible distinction, since the corporate external church is the church as we see it—all of those who

41

"go to church"—and true or spiritually minded believers are, in his words, "all those individuals who personally have become saved"—or, in other words, all those who are God's children by grace, as they are found both in heaven above and on earth below.[17] Because being a child of grace involves a real change in heart and only God can see our hearts (see 1 Kings 8:39), we cannot now know for certain who really are God's children by grace. Thus, the church, in this sense, really is invisible to us. And so when Camping declares that God is no longer blessing and using local churches, that the end of the church age has come, that the institutional church should now disband and its clerical ministries cease, and that true Christians should now in obedience to God remove themselves from their local churches and no longer submit to any ecclesiastical authority, he is in effect declaring that God and his Spirit have forsaken the visible church—that is, the church as it appears in time and space.

We assume that Camping would still affirm that the church is the body of Christ but that he would qualify that statement by saying that it is only the invisible church—composed only of true believers—that is his body. The visible or local church—what Camping calls the corporate external church—is no longer, according to him, to be considered Christ's body.

Yet is this how "the body of Christ" is used in the New Testament? Does it refer exclusively to the invisible church? No, it does not! For example, Paul declares to the local body of believers found in Corinth, "You are the body of Christ" (1 Cor. 12:27). And certainly in Corinth, of all places, we have no reason to assume that every person who was part of that local body was among those who really are children of grace.[18] Camping's distinction between the corporate external church and (relatively) pure fellowships of true or spiritually minded believers is not, then, a biblical distinction.

Moreover, Paul's development of this metaphor of the church as "the body of Christ" works directly against Camping's claim that true believers should leave their local churches to form fellowships that have no church officers. For immediately after declaring to the Corinthians that "you are the body of Christ and individually members of it," Paul continues, "And God has appointed in the church first apostles, second prophets, third teachers, then miracles, then gifts of healing, helping, administrating, and various kinds of tongues" (1 Cor. 12:28). Here, in addition to extraordinary offices like apostleship, are the ordinary church offices of teaching, helping, and administrating—offices that elsewhere in the New Testament we are told are filled by elders and deacons (see 1 Tim. 3:1–13; 5:17; Titus 1:5–9).[19] Those who fill these offices are, of course, among the "many members" of the one body of Christ (1 Cor. 12:12); and Paul in this Corinthian letter goes out of his way to stress that although these many members of the one body are different and thus have diverse functions, this diversity of body "parts" is indispensable to the body's proper functioning:

> The body does not consist of one member but of many. If the foot should say, "Because I am not a hand, I do not belong to the body," that would not make it any less a part of the body. And if the ear should say, "Because I am not an eye, I do not belong to the body," that would not make it any less a part of the body. If the whole body were an eye, where would be the sense of hearing? If the whole body were an ear, where would be the sense of smell? But as it is, God arranged the members in the body, each one of them, as he

chose. . . . As it is, there are many parts, yet one body. (1 Cor. 12:14–20)

He then explicitly draws the consequence that Camping needs to heed: "The eye cannot say to the hand, 'I have no need of you,' nor again the head to the feet, 'I have no need of you' " (1 Cor. 12:21). Each member of the body of Christ is profoundly interdependent on the others—so much so, in fact, that even "the parts of the body that seem to be weaker are indispensable" to its proper functioning (1 Cor. 12:22).

This point that Christ's body—that is, the church—must have an articulated structure including church officers is so important that Paul repeats it three more times in other epistles. In Ephesians, after declaring that Jews and Gentiles are now "members of the same body" (Eph. 3:6), he states that Christ has given to this one body "the apostles, the prophets, the evangelists, the pastors and teachers, to equip the saints for the work of ministry, for building up the body of Christ" (Eph. 4:11–12). Then, a few verses later, he develops this picture of the church as the body of Christ in a way that stresses that the church needs these diverse offices to function properly if it is to flourish. We—that is, the church—

are to grow up in every way into him who is the head, into Christ, from whom the whole body, joined and held together by every joint with which it is equipped, when each part is working properly, makes the body grow so that it builds itself up in love. (Eph. 4:15–16)

He makes much the same point in Romans when he says:

For as in one body we have many members, and the members do not all have the same function, so we, though many, are one body in Christ, and individually members one of another. Having gifts that differ according to the grace given to us, let us use them: if prophecy, in proportion to our faith; if service, in our serving; the one who teaches, in his teaching; the one who exhorts, in his exhortation; the one who contributes, in generosity; the one who leads, with zeal; the one who does acts of mercy, with cheerfulness. (Rom. 12:4–8)

Then, in Colossians, he emphasizes again that Christ's body has—and needs to have—diverse parts when he urges the Colossians to hold fast to Christ, "the Head, from whom the whole body, nourished and knit together through its joints and ligaments, grows with a growth that is from God" (Col. 2:19).

By urging Christians to leave their local churches and form fellowships of believers that have no church officers—no elders, no deacons, and no pastors—Camping is urging us to ignore a basic truth about what a body is and how bodies must function: A body is an articulated structure of diverse parts, each having a specific function that it must carry out for the health of the whole body. When we are speaking of Christ's body, the church, we should recognize that some of those functions—such as those carried out by elders, pastors, and teachers—are ruling functions. Leveling these functions so that "no individuals will have spiritual rule over the congregation,"[20] as Camping's counsel for us to forsake our churches and meet only in believers' fellowships requires, would in effect destroy Christ's body by throwing all its parts into an undifferentiated heap. Nothing in Scripture suggests that we ought to do any such thing.

45

From the "Already" to the "Not Yet"

It would be possible for us to go much further in developing the biblical case against Camping's teaching that the church age is over and that we should all leave our churches to join fellowships of true believers who answer to no one but him.[21] We could learn much more, for instance, from examining the Scriptures that portray the church as Christ's bride, as God's building, as the earthly outpost of God's kingdom, as God's family and God's flock, and so on.

We do not deny that there is much about the church as we experience it that is distressing and, were it not for God's promise never to forsake her, we might wonder whether he had abandoned his bride. Yet Scripture encourages us not to lose heart but to trust God's promises. Camping's claim that the church age is over is not only unbiblical but ultimately a counsel of despair. God has promised us, as his body, that he will never leave us nor forsake us; and his Spirit, in spite of Camping's claims to the contrary, has not left his people, nor will he ever do so!

The church, as we now see her, is already God's people, but she is not yet glorified. Yet God is surely and certainly moving her toward that glorification by his own appointed means. Those means are the constant preaching and teaching of his Word, regular observance of his sacraments, and unceasing prayer—all in the context of mutual accountability and pastoral discipline that his gift to us of pastors, elders, and deacons provides. As the church does what God has commanded for her to do—to worship,[22] to fellowship, to discipline, to serve, and to witness—God is already fashioning his whole people, as they participate in local congregations, into the still-to-be-revealed glorified body of Christ.

It is in looking forward to this glorification—and not in looking for signs that we are now in the end times—that we must anchor our lives and our hope. And it is in doing this that we shall begin to see the church, as imperfect and incomplete as she currently is, for what she shall become. Already she is God's people, Christ's body, his bride, his building, the earthly outpost of his kingdom, his family, and his flock. But she is not yet the glorious being she shall become. Eric Alexander helps us, during this time between the times, to look beyond her current blemishes to anticipate the beauty of what she will become:

Glorification . . . gives a new, true, biblical sense of perspective to our view of the world and of history. We need to ask ourselves, "What is the really important thing that is happening in the world in our generation? Where are the really significant events taking place? Are they taking place in the seats of government and power here in London or Washington or Beijing or wherever? What is the most important thing? Where do you need to look in the modern world to see the most significant event from a divine perspective? Where is the focus of God's activity in history?" In answer to all these questions, the most significant thing happening in history is the calling, redeeming and perfecting of the people of God. God is building the church of Jesus Christ. The rest of history is simply a stage God erects for that purpose. He is calling out a people. He is perfecting them. He is changing them. History's great climax comes when God brings down the curtain on this bankrupt world and the Lord Jesus Christ arrives in his infinite glory. The rest of history is simply the scaffolding for the real work.

The last time I was in London, the front of [the] great Abbey of Westminster was covered in scaffolding as they were cleaning it. They were beautifying it. They were preparing it for a future day. One could not see its true beauty, but one was aware that something of great significance was happening behind that web of scaffolding. Something of majestic beauty was to be revealed. The same thing is happening in my own city of Glasgow. Some of its magnificent Victorian buildings are covered months and even years with scaffolding. Then, when the scaffolding is taken down, the architecture is revealed in all its pristine glory.

There will come a day when God will pull down the scaffolding of world history. Do you know what he will be pointing to when he says to the whole creation, "There is my masterpiece"? He will be pointing to the church of Jesus Christ. In the forefront of it all will be the Lord Jesus himself who will come and say, "Here am I, and the children you have given me, perfected in the beauty of holiness."

That is the day for which we are laboring.[23]

Isn't that astounding? And Camping completely misses it! The church is not incidental to God's purposes in history but absolutely central. The glorification of his body, his people, his building, is at the heart of his plan of redemption.

We urge those of you who have been influenced by Camping's unbiblical teaching to rethink your commitment to what is, in fact, a profoundly un-Christian vision of God's church. Christ has not abandoned, nor will he ever abandon, his bride. Those who encourage us to slight her will come under his judgment on the last day. Indeed, we pray for Harold Camping and plead with him to return to Scripture's true doctrine of Christ's church.

FOR FURTHER STUDY

All of this sad business should motivate us as evangelicals to study the church. We recommend the following books for a thorough study of the biblical doctrine of the church: Edmund P. Clowney, The Church (Downers Grove, Ill.: InterVarsity, 1995); James Bannerman, The Church of Christ (Edinburgh: Banner of Truth, 1974); D. Douglas Bannerman, The Scripture Doctrine of the Church (Grand Rapids: Baker, 1976); and Mark Dever, Nine Marks of a Healthy Church, rev. ed. (Wheaton, Ill.: Crossway, 2000).

NOTES

Introduction

1. See Harold Camping, 1994? (New York: Vantage, 1992). As the question mark in the title signifies, Camping admits in his introduction that "even though I am quite certain that all of these signs point to the end of time being very close, the possibility does exist that I could be wrong"; he immediately goes on to say, though, that "such a possibility appears to be quite remote" (xv). Considering that Camping's prediction has been unfulfilled for nearly ten years, he has certainly demonstrated that his methods of biblical interpretation are unreliable.

2. Other than criticizing the doctrine of baptismal regeneration, Camping said nothing explicitly about the sacraments of baptism and the Lord's Supper in his paper "Has the Era of the Church Age Come to an End?" which appeared on the Family Radio website. That paper has been replaced by The End of the Church Age . . . and After, an online book (see www.familyradio.com and follow the links

under "Literature") that explicitly affirms the cessation of sacraments (p. 236). Since Christ gave these ordinances to the visible church, we may assume that they ought not to be practiced in Camping's fellowships any more than the ordinances given to Israel by God were meant to continue after the temple was destroyed. Camping has confirmed this in conversation on Open Forum. See James R. White, *Dangerous Airwaves: Harold Camping Refuted and Christ's Church Defended* (Amityville, N.Y.: Calvary, 2000), 124–30.

3. *End of the Church Age*, p. 260–61.

4. See our statement at www.christianity.com/ace.

Chapter 1

1. www.familyradio.com.

2. *End of the Church Age*, p. 283.

3. Now, don't be confused by this! Christians have always distinguished between what the Reformers called "the visible and the invisible church" (although other Christians did this in different ways and often with different terms). That is, Christians have always acknowledged that there is an invisible communion of the saints that transcends time and place and culture and even death. This—the church universal—consists of all who are God's children by grace, as they are found both in heaven above and on earth below. We also affirm that there is a visible church on earth consisting of believers and their children. Yet the Reformers did not attempt to pit the one against the other. They did not postulate a radical discontinuity between the visible and the invisible church. God intends for his church to be visible; and so a believer's connection to and membership in that visible church is vital. But Camping has sundered the visible church with its divinely given orders

and ordinances (ministers, elders, deacons, sacraments, commission, government, discipline, etc.) from the invisible church with its individual members. According to him, the former has ceased while the latter continues.

4. End of the Church Age, p. 74.

5. Ibid., p. 78.

6. Ibid., p. 79.

7. Ibid., p. 259–60.

Chapter 2

1. For a longer response, see White's Dangerous Airwaves.

2. John Piper, Let the Nations Be Glad! The Supremacy of God in Missions, 2d ed. (Grand Rapids: Baker, 2003), p.17.

3. For a proper, incarnational view, see Paul's great statements in 2 Cor. 4–5.

4. Christians have long distinguished between God's revealed will and his secret will on the basis of verses like Deut. 29:29: "The secret things belong to the LORD our God, but the things that are revealed belong to us and to our children forever, that we may do all the words of this law." As this verse suggests, God reveals what he wants us to believe and to do. But in general, he keeps secret what he has ordained to happen. By having claimed in the past to know the year in which Christ would return as well as now claiming to know that we are in the Great Tribulation, Camping is claiming to be privy to God's secret will. He would do much better to study what Scripture reveals about how God wills for believers to relate to him and each other through his church.

5. Camping's exegesis is allegorical because it takes particular words in Scripture always to bear the same meaning. For instance, in End of the Church Age (p. 228), we read that "Jerusalem or Judea represent all of the New Testament

churches and denominations" (with particular reference to Luke 21:20–24), that "The mountain or mountains are a reference of God being our help" (interpreting the same passage in Luke), and that "The housetop is identified with bringing the Gospel" (interpreting Luke 17:31). To be sure, there is more to Camping's prophetic exegesis than this sort of allegorical interpretation, but this sort of allegorical interpretation of Scripture, which was rejected by the magisterial Reformers at the start of the Protestant Reformation, is central to Camping's argument.

For a much fuller critique of Camping's allegorical method, see White's Dangerous Airwaves. White shows that if we apply Camping's allegorical method of interpretation to his own writings, we can come up with conclusions that he would repudiate. This demonstrates that any such method of interpreting someone's writings is unreliable at best.

6. Gnosticism is an error that has plagued the church from ancient times. Early Christian theologians such as Irenaeus, Tertullian, Hippolytus, and Epiphanius condemned the Gnostics (who were so called from the Greek word for "knowledge," that is, gnosis) for leading Christians astray by claiming that there are deep, hidden meanings to the Scriptures that can be discovered only (often by allegorical interpretation) by those who are especially "spiritual." Camping has both said and implied that he is especially qualified to discover such meanings because of (among other things) the special way that he reads the Scriptures due to his training as an engineer. Yet already in Ephesians, Paul warns his readers not to let anyone deceive them with "empty words" (Eph. 5:6), and later, in his pastoral epistles, he condemns "quarrels about words, which produce envy, dissension, slander, evil suspicions, and constant friction among people who are depraved in mind and deprived

of the truth" (1 Tim. 6:4–5; cf. 6:3–5; 2 Tim. 2:14, 2; Titus 3:9–11). Peter is also concerned to confront and combat Gnostic tendencies in his second letter.

Chapter 3

1. In the Old Testament, Israelites alone are referred to as God's children and called his people—in other words, in the Old Testament, Israelites alone are God's "family." For instance, at Deuteronomy 14:1–2 Moses says, "You are the sons of the LORD your God. You shall not cut yourselves or make any baldness on your foreheads for the dead. For you are a people holy to the LORD your God, and the LORD has chosen you to be a people for his treasured possession, out of all the peoples who are on the face of the earth." In the New Testament, "all who are led by the Spirit of God are sons of God" (Rom. 8:14). Paul calls the Holy Spirit "the Spirit of adoption" by whom believers know that they are God's own sons and daughters, and "by whom we cry, 'Abba! Father!' " (Rom. 8:15). "The Spirit himself," Paul says, "bears witness with our spirit that we are children of God, and if children, then heirs—heirs of God and fellow heirs with Christ" (Rom. 8:16–17). Paul is at pains, in more than one place in his letters, to make clear that this means that believing Gentiles, as well as Jews, are now part of the family of God (see Rom. 9:26 with Hos. 1:10; Gal. 3:26–4:7).

2. The English word "session" is derived from the Latin word sessio, which means "to sit." Other biblical references to Christ's heavenly session include Mark 14:62; Rom. 8:34; Col. 3:1; Heb. 8:1; 10:12; 12:2; and 1 Peter 3:22.

3. John Calvin, Institutes of the Christian Religion (Louisville: Westminster John Knox, 1960), 1:524 (Book II, xvi, 15). While Calvin rightly stresses that the heavenly ses-

sion of Christ is primarily concerned with the risen Christ's kingly office, Scripture also links it to his priestly (see Zech. 6:13; Heb. 4:14–16; 7:24–25; 8:1–6; 9:24) and prophetical (see John 14:26; 16:7–15) offices.

4. Scripture warrants our saying that the greatest gift that the seated Christ has given to his disciples is the gift of the Holy Spirit (see Acts 2:33, 38 and 10:45 along with John 15:26 and 16:7). The Holy Spirit is, then, spoken of as making some "overseers" to the church (see Acts 20:28). So Christ gives to his body the gift of church officers through the gift of his Spirit.

5. Paul explicitly says that Christ's gift of apostles, prophets, evangelists, pastors, and teachers is "for building up the body of Christ" (Eph. 4:12), and he urges the Corinthians to seek those manifestations of the Spirit that will build up the church (1 Cor. 14:12). See also Acts 14:23; 20:28; 1 Tim. 3:1–5; 2 Tim. 2:2; Titus 1:5–9; 2:1–15; Heb. 13:17.

6. Paul distinguishes between the Corinthians' simply assembling together and their assembling together "as a church" (see 1 Cor. 11:18–22). Given the fact that baptism and the Lord's Supper are assumed to be ordinances that all believers observe (see Matt. 28:19, Mark 16:16, Rom. 6:2–5, and Col. 2:12 for baptism and Matt. 28:20 with Luke 22:19 and 1 Cor. 11:23–26 for the Lord's Supper), we can assume that to assemble as a church means to assemble, at least in part, to share in the sacraments and thus to "proclaim the Lord's death until he comes" (1 Cor. 11:26). In fact, the apostle Paul suggests that partaking in the Lord's Supper is what unifies us as a church body: "The cup of blessing that we bless, is it not a participation in the blood of Christ? The bread that we break, is it not a participation in the body of Christ? Because there is one bread, we who are many are

one body, for we all partake of the one bread" (1 Cor. 10:16–17). We can also assume from what is actually said in Scripture that every church has ordained elders who preach and teach and guide, care for, and discipline their flocks (see Acts 14:23; Titus 1:5; James 5:14; 1 Peter 5:1–5).

7. These passages remind us that the visible church, according to Scripture, will be imperfect until Christ returns. Discipline cannot create a perfect church. Note that Protestant paedo-baptists view the visible church as consisting of believers and their children, while Baptists believe that the visible church comprises believers only.

8. For more on the biblical "marks of the church," see Mark Dever, Nine Marks of a Healthy Church (Wheaton, Ill.: Crossway, 2000). See note 6, above, for Scriptures to support the claim that believers are always to be part of churches that are governed by ordained elders, pastors, teachers, and that administer the sacraments.

9. See note 1, above.

10. For the Scriptures that support this, see note 6, above.

11. Bruce Milne, Know the Truth (Downers Grove, Ill., InterVarsity Press, 1999), p. 210.

12. Heb. 8:8–13 quotes Jer. 31:31–34 in its entirety in order to make clear that God has now in this New Testament era fulfilled his Old Testament promise.

13. As we have already observed in Chapter 2 (point 10), the New Testament recognizes a two-stage realization of this fulfillment—the "already" of our present full and unconditional acceptance with God because of Christ's finished work and the "not yet" of our final perfection in Christ when our obedience will become perfect.

14. These promises are part of what is known in Reformed theology as "the covenant of redemption," which is a covenant among the three persons of the Trinity. It is the

eternal basis of the covenant of grace. For more on these covenants, see Louis Berkhof, Systematic Theology (Grand Rapids: Eerdmans, 1938), pp. 262–301, and Wayne Grudem, Systematic Theology (Grand Rapids: Zondervan, 1994), pp. 515–22.

15. This assumption is profoundly un-Christian in the sense that it refuses to acknowledge the profound effects that Christ's finished work has on the way God relates to his new covenant people.

16. Paul's imagery here is a little fluid. For instance, sometimes he speaks of Christ's body with us as its members (see 1 Cor. 10:16; Rom. 12:5), and sometimes he refers to Christ as the head and us as the body (see Col. 1:18; 2:19).

17. As we have already noted, there are legitimate, biblically faithful ways to make and use this distinction between the visible and the invisible church; but Camping's way of making and using it is not among them.

18. The New Testament writers never assume that all who are in the church are children of grace. As John puts it, it is only as people go out from us that it becomes plain that they are not of us (see 1 John 2:18–19). Yet Christ's parable about the wheat and the weeds makes it clear that we ourselves are not to try to purge the church of "all causes of sin and all law-breakers" (Matt. 13:41; cf. vv. 24–30 and vv. 36–43). In fact, Christ explicitly commands his disciples: "Let both [weeds and wheat] grow together until the harvest" (Matt. 13:30)—that is, until Christ's return. He will then send angels to gather out of his kingdom all those who are not true children of grace. In urging "true" or "spiritually minded" believers to leave their local churches and form "fellowships," Camping is urging us to carry out this sorting process ourselves, which directly violates Christ's command.

19. For the distinction between extraordinary and ordinary church offices, see Berkhof's Systematic Theology, pp. 585–87. For a rather different interpretation of the same Scriptures, see Grudem's Systematic Theology, pp. 905–20.

20. End of the Church Age, p. 260.

21. It is ironic, given Camping's claim that no one is any longer supposed to exercise spiritual rule over God's people, that Camping functions as the de facto spiritual leader of all those who hearken to his erroneous teaching. One evening spent listening to Open Forum clearly establishes that "Brother Camping" is taken to be first among the brothers.

22. Worship includes the faithful reading, preaching, praying, and singing of God's Word and the right administration of his sacraments.

23. Eric J. Alexander, "The Application of Redemption," in To Glorify and Enjoy God, eds. John L. Carson and David W. Hall (Edinburgh: Banner of Truth, 1994), pp. 245–46.

J. Ligon Duncan (M.Div., M.A., Covenant Theological Seminary; Ph.D., University of Edinburgh) is the senior minister of the historic First Presbyterian Church in Jackson, Mississippi, and was formerly the John R. Richardson professor of systematic theology at Reformed Theological Seminary. He serves on the Council on Biblical Manhood and Womanhood and the Alliance of Confessing Evangelicals.

Mark R. Talbot (Ph.D., University of Pennsylvania) is associate professor of philosophy at Wheaton College. He is vice-chair of the Council of the Alliance of Confessing Evangelicals and executive editor of Modern Reformation magazine. Talbot is the author of The Signs of True Conversion and many articles, and speaks internationally.